Stock Crash

Full details of The US Stock Fall And Effects On The World Economy

By

Barbs Walters

Copyright © 2024, by Barbs Walters.

All rights reserved. No part of this book may be reproduced or transmitted in any form or by any means, electronic or mechanical, including photocopying, recording, or any information storage and retrieval system, without permission in writing from the copyright owner, except for brief quotations in critical reviews and articles.

Table Of Contents

Copyright © 2024, by Barbs Walters.   **1**

Chapter 1: Introduction to the Global Market Tumble 4

   Overview of Recent Market Events   4

   Key Players and Indices Affected   6

   Initial Reactions and Market Sentiment   7

Chapter 2: Economic Indicators and Their Impact   13

   U.S. Jobs Data: A Catalyst for Concern   13

   The Role of Central Banks and Interest Rates   16

   Inflation and Currency Fluctuations   20

Chapter 3: Technology Sector: Overvaluation and Uncertainty   25

   The Rise and Fall of Big Tech Stocks   25

   The AI Boom: Opportunities and Risks   28

   Case Studies: Nvidia, Intel, Amazon, and Apple   32

Chapter 4: Global Ripple Effects   38

   Market Reactions in Europe and Asia   38

   The Strengthening Yen and Japan's Economic Challenges   41

   Contagion Fears: A Global Perspective   45

Chapter 5: Investors' Reactions and Strategies   50

   Short-Term vs. Long-Term Investor Behavior   50

   The Role of Institutional Investors   55

   Mitigation Strategies in a Volatile Market   60

Chapter 6: Analyzing the U.S. Economic Outlook   65

   Growth Prospects and Recession Risks   65

   The Federal Reserve's Dilemma   70

Economic Policy and Political Factors 75
Chapter 7: Comparative Analysis: Global Economic Health **80**
Comparing Major Economies: U.S., Europe, Asia 80
Central Bank Policies Across the Globe 87
The Role of Trade and Geopolitical Tensions 92
Chapter 8: Lessons Learned and Future Predictions 97
Historical Comparisons: Previous Market Crashes 97
What Investors Can Learn from the Recent Tumble 102
Future Market Trends and Predictions 107

Chapter 1: Introduction to the Global Market Tumble

Overview of Recent Market Events

The global financial landscape has recently been rocked by a series of sharp downturns across major stock markets. This chapter delves into the precipitating factors and the cascading effects that have characterized this period of instability. The confluence of various economic signals and global events has created a tumultuous environment, causing widespread concern among investors, policymakers, and the general public.

The initial signs of turbulence were observed in the United States, where stock indices experienced significant losses. The technology-heavy Nasdaq, which has been a bellwether for market sentiment due to its concentration of high-growth tech stocks, opened 6.3% lower following a sharp decline at the close of the previous week. While it managed to pare some losses by the end of the day, the damage was already done, setting the tone for a broader market downturn.

This downturn was not confined to American shores. European markets, too, felt the impact, with major indices such as the CAC-40 in Paris, Frankfurt's DAX, and the UK's FTSE 100 all recording significant declines. In Asia, the situation was equally grim. Japan's Nikkei 225 plunged by approximately 12.4%, its most substantial drop in recent memory, while markets in Taiwan, South Korea, India, Australia, Hong Kong, and Shanghai also suffered steep declines ranging from 1.4% to 8%.

Key Players and Indices Affected

The primary indices affected by this downturn are representative of the broader economic landscape. The Dow Jones Industrial Average, which includes 30 of the largest publicly traded companies in the United States, fell by 2.6%. This index is often viewed as a barometer of the overall health of the American economy, making its decline particularly concerning. The S&P 500, which encompasses a broader range of 500 companies across various industries, also dropped by 3%, highlighting the widespread nature of the market downturn.

In the technology sector, several high-profile companies experienced notable declines. Nvidia, a leading producer of graphics processing units (GPUs) and a key player in the burgeoning field of artificial intelligence (AI), saw its shares drop by 6.3%. This decline was particularly significant given Nvidia's recent prominence as a market leader in AI technology. Similarly, Amazon, a global e-commerce giant and a key player in cloud computing, fell by 4.1%. Apple, another tech behemoth, also saw its stock decline by 4.8%, underscoring the vulnerability of even the most established companies in the face of market volatility.

The impact of these declines was not limited to the tech sector. Other industries also felt the effects, with significant losses observed across a wide range of sectors. This broad-based decline indicates a general apprehension among investors about the economic outlook, rather than concerns confined to specific industries or companies.

Initial Reactions and Market Sentiment

The immediate reaction to the market downturn was one of alarm and uncertainty. Investors, who had enjoyed a period of relative stability and growth, were suddenly faced with the possibility of a prolonged period of economic difficulty. The weak jobs data from the United States, which revealed that only 114,000 roles were added in July, far below expectations, exacerbated these fears. The unemployment rate also ticked up from 4.1% to 4.3%, adding to concerns that the long-running jobs boom in the U.S. might be coming to an end.

This data sparked widespread speculation about the future course of the U.S. economy. Some analysts suggested that the weak jobs numbers could be a one-off event, possibly influenced by external factors such as Hurricane Beryl, a Category 5 storm that hit parts of the Gulf Coast. However, others warned that this could be an early sign of a broader economic slowdown, particularly given the Federal Reserve's recent decision to hold off on cutting interest rates. The central bank's reluctance to reduce rates, in contrast to other central banks such as the Bank of England, added to the uncertainty, as lower rates typically encourage economic growth by making borrowing cheaper.

The market's initial response was also colored by concerns about the valuation of technology stocks, particularly those heavily invested in artificial intelligence. Over the past few years, companies in this sector have seen their valuations soar, driven by the promise of revolutionary advancements in AI technology. However, the recent downturn has led to questions about whether these valuations were overly optimistic. The announcement of major layoffs at Intel, another key player in the technology sector, and disappointing financial results added to these concerns. There was also speculation that Nvidia might delay the launch of its latest AI chip, further dampening investor sentiment.

In Europe, the market reaction was similarly cautious. The declines in major indices such as the

CAC-40, DAX, and FTSE 100 reflected broader concerns about the global economic outlook. The European Central Bank's cautious stance on monetary policy, amid a mixed economic picture across the continent, added to the uncertainty. In Japan, the strengthening of the yen against the U.S. dollar, following the Bank of Japan's decision to raise interest rates, created additional challenges for the country's export-oriented economy. A stronger yen makes Japanese goods more expensive for foreign buyers, potentially hurting sales and profits for Japanese companies.

Amidst these developments, the narrative of a potential global slowdown gained traction. While some market participants remained hopeful that the downturn would be short-lived, others feared that it could be the beginning of a more extended period of economic difficulty. The specter of a global recession, though not yet a certainty, loomed large over the markets. This uncertainty was compounded by geopolitical tensions, trade disputes, and other external factors that could potentially exacerbate the economic situation.

The initial market sentiment was characterized by a mix of fear, uncertainty, and cautious optimism. While the declines in stock prices were undoubtedly alarming, some investors viewed them as a potential buying opportunity, betting that the markets would recover in the medium to long term. Others, however, adopted a more defensive posture, reallocating assets to safer investments such as government bonds or gold, which traditionally hold value in times of economic uncertainty.

The recent market tumble represents a significant moment in the global financial landscape. The convergence of weak economic data, concerns about overvaluation in the technology sector, and broader geopolitical uncertainties have created a challenging environment for investors. As the situation continues to unfold, it will be crucial to monitor these developments and their potential impact on the global economy. The initial reactions and market sentiment captured in this chapter provide a snapshot of a period of heightened anxiety and uncertainty, setting the stage for a deeper exploration of the factors driving these market dynamics in the subsequent chapters.

Chapter 2: Economic Indicators and Their Impact

U.S. Jobs Data: A Catalyst for Concern

In the intricate world of economics, data on employment figures often serves as a crucial indicator of a country's economic health. Recently, the United States released a report revealing unexpectedly weak job growth, which sent ripples through global financial markets. This section delves into the implications of these figures and how they acted as a trigger for broader concerns about the U.S. and global economies.

The reported addition of 114,000 jobs in July was significantly below market expectations. This underperformance marked a stark deviation from the steady job gains observed over the past several months. Coupled with an uptick in the unemployment rate from 4.1% to 4.3%, these numbers painted a less optimistic picture of the labor market. The U.S. labor market has been a linchpin of economic resilience, consistently absorbing shocks from various sectors. However, the latest data hinted at potential vulnerabilities, prompting analysts and investors to question the sustainability of this trend.

Several factors may have contributed to the disappointing job growth. One possible explanation is the lingering impact of Hurricane Beryl, a severe storm that disrupted activities in parts of the Gulf Coast. Natural disasters often lead to temporary disruptions in hiring and economic activity, and it remains uncertain whether this event played a significant role in the reported figures.

Alternatively, the data could reflect broader structural issues within the economy, such as a mismatch between the skills required by employers and those possessed by job seekers, or a decline in labor force participation rates.

Beyond the headline numbers, the composition of job gains also raised eyebrows. The sectors traditionally viewed as stable sources of employment, such as healthcare and professional services, showed slower growth. Meanwhile, industries like retail and hospitality, often seen as more volatile, contributed a larger share of new jobs. This shift in the composition of job gains could indicate underlying shifts in the economy, with potential implications for wage growth and consumer spending.

The reaction to the jobs report was swift and pronounced. Investors, already jittery from other economic signals, interpreted the data as a sign that the U.S. economy might be losing momentum. The immediate consequence was a sell-off in equities, as market participants adjusted their expectations for future economic growth. Moreover, the weak job numbers fueled speculation about the Federal Reserve's future actions, particularly concerning interest rate policy, which brings us to the next critical aspect of this chapter.

The Role of Central Banks and Interest Rates

Central banks play a pivotal role in managing economic stability, primarily through their control of interest rates and monetary policy. The U.S. Federal Reserve, in particular, is closely watched by global markets, as its decisions can have far-reaching implications. In the context of the recent market downturn, the Fed's stance on interest rates became a focal point of discussion.

In the days leading up to the market turmoil, the Federal Reserve opted to maintain the current interest rate levels, resisting calls for a rate cut. This decision stood in contrast to other central banks, such as the Bank of England, which had adopted a more accommodative stance. The Fed's choice was influenced by a complex interplay of factors, including inflation, employment data, and overall economic growth.

One of the primary considerations for the Federal Reserve in setting interest rates is the balance between stimulating economic growth and controlling inflation. Lower interest rates typically encourage borrowing and investment, which can spur economic activity. However, they also carry the risk of overheating the economy, leading to rising prices. Conversely, higher rates can help contain inflation but may also dampen economic growth by making borrowing more expensive.

The recent weak jobs data complicated the Fed's calculus. On one hand, slower job growth and rising unemployment suggested a cooling economy, which might argue for lower rates to stimulate growth. On the other hand, inflationary pressures remained a concern, particularly with recent increases in the prices of goods and services. The Fed's decision to hold rates steady indicated a cautious approach, seeking to strike a balance between these competing pressures.

The market reaction to the Fed's decision was mixed. Some investors were disappointed, hoping for a rate cut that would provide a boost to economic activity and stock prices. Others viewed the decision as a prudent measure to prevent inflation from getting out of control. The ambiguity in the Fed's future actions added to market uncertainty, with analysts closely scrutinizing future statements and economic data for clues about the central bank's next moves.

Globally, other central banks faced similar dilemmas. The European Central Bank (ECB), for instance, has been navigating a complex economic environment characterized by sluggish growth and low inflation. The ECB's cautious approach mirrored that of the Fed, as it balanced the need for economic stimulus with concerns about financial stability. Meanwhile, the Bank of Japan faced unique challenges related to a strong yen and persistent deflationary pressures, complicating its policy choices.

The interplay between central bank policies and market reactions underscores the importance of clear communication and careful calibration of monetary policy. In times of economic uncertainty, central banks' decisions can either stabilize or exacerbate market volatility, depending on how they are perceived by investors and the public.

Inflation and Currency Fluctuations

Inflation and currency fluctuations are interrelated phenomena that can significantly impact economies and financial markets. In recent months, both have been at the forefront of economic discussions, particularly in the context of the United States and other major economies.

Inflation refers to the rate at which the general level of prices for goods and services rises, eroding purchasing power. In the U.S., inflation has been a topic of concern, with consumer prices rising at a faster pace than expected. Several factors have contributed to this trend, including supply chain disruptions, rising energy prices, and increased consumer demand as the economy recovers from the pandemic. These inflationary pressures have posed a challenge for the Federal Reserve, as it seeks to balance the dual mandate of promoting maximum employment and stable prices.

In Japan, inflationary dynamics have been different. The country has long struggled with low inflation and occasional deflation, where prices decline over time. However, recent data showed a rise in inflation, exceeding expectations. This unexpected increase complicated the Bank of Japan's efforts to achieve its inflation target while also supporting economic growth. The stronger yen, which appreciated following the Bank's interest rate hike, added another layer of complexity. A stronger currency makes exports more expensive and less competitive, potentially hurting the export-driven Japanese economy.

Currency fluctuations, such as the recent appreciation of the yen, are influenced by a variety of factors, including interest rate differentials, economic data, and geopolitical developments. In the current environment, currency movements have been particularly pronounced, reflecting the uncertainty and volatility in global markets. The U.S. dollar, for example, has experienced fluctuations against a basket of currencies, influenced by changing expectations about Federal Reserve policy and economic conditions.

These currency movements have significant implications for trade and investment flows. For exporters, a stronger domestic currency can make their goods more expensive in foreign markets, potentially reducing demand. Conversely, importers may benefit from a stronger currency, as it makes foreign goods cheaper. For investors, currency fluctuations can affect the returns on international investments, adding another layer of risk to an already complex landscape.

In addition to the economic implications, inflation and currency fluctuations can also influence consumer behavior and business decisions. Rising prices can erode consumer purchasing power, leading to changes in spending patterns. Businesses, facing higher costs for raw materials and labor, may need to adjust their pricing strategies, potentially passing on costs to consumers. These dynamics can create a feedback loop, where inflation expectations influence actual inflation outcomes, further complicating the task of central banks.

In summary, the recent market tumble has brought to the forefront a range of economic indicators, each with its own set of implications for the global economy. The weak U.S. jobs data, central bank policies, and inflationary pressures have all contributed to a complex and uncertain environment. As we move forward, the interplay between these factors will continue to shape market dynamics and economic outcomes. The next chapters will explore these themes in greater detail, examining their impact on different sectors and regions, and considering the potential paths forward for the global economy.

Chapter 3: Technology Sector: Overvaluation and Uncertainty

The Rise and Fall of Big Tech Stocks

The technology sector has been a central force in the global economy, driving innovation, shaping consumer behavior, and contributing significantly to stock market growth. In recent years, big tech companies have enjoyed a meteoric rise, with valuations soaring to unprecedented levels. However, this upward trajectory has not been without its pitfalls, as recent market fluctuations have revealed vulnerabilities and prompted concerns about overvaluation.

The ascent of technology stocks was fueled by a confluence of factors. The proliferation of digital platforms, the increasing reliance on cloud computing, and the transformative potential of artificial intelligence (AI) have all played pivotal roles in elevating the sector. Companies like Apple, Amazon, and Alphabet (Google's parent company) became titans of industry, boasting market capitalizations in the trillions. The narrative of boundless growth, underpinned by continuous technological advancement, attracted a flood of investor capital, further propelling stock prices.

However, the rapid appreciation in the value of these stocks also led to an environment ripe for speculative excess. Valuations were often justified by optimistic projections of future earnings, sometimes disconnected from the companies' current financial performance. Price-to-earnings ratios in the tech sector reached dizzying heights, sparking debates among analysts about whether these valuations were sustainable or if a bubble was forming.

The recent market downturn has brought these concerns into sharp focus. As broader economic indicators began to flash warning signs, investors started reassessing their positions, leading to a significant sell-off in tech stocks. The Nasdaq, a key index dominated by technology companies, experienced a notable decline, highlighting the sector's vulnerability to shifts in market sentiment. The sell-off was not limited to lesser-known firms but also affected industry giants, underscoring the pervasive uncertainty that had gripped the market.

Several factors contributed to the decline. First, the macroeconomic environment became increasingly challenging. Concerns about rising interest rates, inflation, and slowing economic growth created a backdrop of heightened uncertainty. Higher interest rates, in particular, are often detrimental to high-growth tech stocks, as they increase the cost of capital and reduce the present value of future earnings. Second, specific events within the tech sector exacerbated the downturn. For instance, disappointing earnings reports, announcements of layoffs, and delays in product launches all served to undermine investor confidence.

The fall in big tech stocks has not only impacted investors but also raised questions about the broader implications for the economy. These companies are not just market darlings; they are also major employers, innovators, and drivers of economic growth. A sustained decline in their stock prices could have ripple effects, potentially dampening investment in new technologies and slowing the pace of innovation.

The AI Boom: Opportunities and Risks

Artificial intelligence has been hailed as the next frontier in technological innovation, with the potential to revolutionize industries and transform everyday life. The AI boom has been characterized by significant investments in research and development, a surge in AI-related startups, and a growing number of applications across various sectors, from healthcare to finance to manufacturing. This enthusiasm has also been reflected in the stock market, where companies involved in AI have seen their valuations soar.

The opportunities presented by AI are vast. In healthcare, AI algorithms are being used to improve diagnostics, personalize treatment plans, and streamline administrative processes. In finance, AI-driven analytics are enhancing risk assessment, fraud detection, and customer service. In manufacturing, AI-powered automation is increasing efficiency and reducing costs. These examples merely scratch the surface of AI's potential, as the technology continues to evolve and find new applications.

However, alongside these opportunities, the AI boom has also brought significant risks. One major concern is the potential for overvaluation. The hype surrounding AI has led to a flood of investment, with companies often receiving lofty valuations based on their AI capabilities or aspirations. In some cases, these valuations may be out of sync with the companies' actual technological capabilities or market prospects. This has raised fears of an AI bubble, where speculative investment outpaces genuine innovation and market demand.

Another risk is the ethical and societal implications of AI. As the technology becomes more pervasive, concerns about privacy, bias, and job displacement have come to the fore. AI systems, particularly those involved in decision-making processes, can sometimes perpetuate or exacerbate biases present in their training data. This can lead to unfair or discriminatory outcomes, raising ethical questions about the use and governance of AI. Moreover, the increasing automation of tasks traditionally performed by humans poses a challenge to the labor market, with potential job losses in certain sectors.

The regulatory landscape for AI is also evolving, adding another layer of uncertainty. Governments and regulatory bodies around the world are grappling with how to oversee the development and deployment of AI technologies. The challenge lies in creating frameworks that encourage innovation while protecting public interests. The lack of clear and consistent regulations can create uncertainty for companies operating in this space, potentially affecting investment and growth.

Despite these risks, the AI boom continues to be a major driver of activity and innovation in the tech sector. Companies are pouring resources into developing AI capabilities, and investors remain eager to back ventures that promise to harness the power of AI. The key for stakeholders will be to navigate the hype and focus on the real, sustainable opportunities that AI presents, while being mindful of the potential pitfalls.

Case Studies: Nvidia, Intel, Amazon, and Apple

To illustrate the dynamics of the technology sector during this period of uncertainty, we turn to four prominent companies: Nvidia, Intel, Amazon, and Apple. Each of these companies has a unique position in the market and has faced distinct challenges and opportunities in the recent market environment.

Nvidia: Nvidia has been at the forefront of the AI revolution, thanks to its powerful graphics processing units (GPUs), which are essential for AI and machine learning tasks. The company's GPUs are widely used in data centers, gaming, and increasingly in automotive applications, such as autonomous vehicles. Nvidia's stock price surged as demand for its products grew, and the company's financial performance was robust. However, the recent market downturn affected Nvidia as well, with its stock price declining amid concerns about overvaluation and broader market conditions.

One specific challenge for Nvidia has been the cyclical nature of demand in some of its key markets, such as gaming. Additionally, geopolitical tensions and trade policies have impacted the semiconductor industry, with potential disruptions in supply chains and access to key markets. Despite these challenges, Nvidia continues to invest in AI and other growth areas, positioning itself as a key player in the next wave of technological innovation.

Intel: Intel, a stalwart in the semiconductor industry, has faced its own set of challenges. The company has been undergoing a strategic shift, aiming to catch up with competitors in advanced manufacturing processes and expand its presence in new markets, such as AI and 5G. However, Intel has encountered delays in its product launches and manufacturing transitions, which have affected its market share and stock performance.

Recently, Intel announced major layoffs and reported disappointing financial results, adding to investor concerns. The company's struggles highlight the competitive pressures in the semiconductor industry and the difficulties of executing a strategic transformation. Nonetheless, Intel's substantial resources and long-standing industry relationships provide it with a foundation to navigate these challenges and potentially capitalize on new opportunities in emerging technologies.

Amazon: Amazon is a behemoth in e-commerce and cloud computing, with its Amazon Web Services (AWS) division being a significant driver of the company's profitability. The pandemic accelerated the shift towards online shopping, benefiting

Amazon's retail operations. However, the post-pandemic normalization of consumer behavior and macroeconomic factors, such as inflation and supply chain disruptions, have created headwinds for the company.

Amazon's stock has experienced volatility, reflecting both the opportunities and risks associated with its business model. The company's significant investments in logistics, AI, and new business ventures, such as healthcare, demonstrate its ambition to remain a dominant player in multiple industries. However, these investments also come with risks, particularly in an uncertain economic environment where consumer spending may be constrained.

Apple: Apple, one of the most valuable companies in the world, has built a strong brand and a loyal customer base through its ecosystem of products and services. The company's financial performance has been robust, with steady revenue growth driven by strong sales of its flagship products, such as the iPhone, as well as growth in its services segment. However, Apple is not immune to broader market dynamics and has faced its own challenges.

The recent decline in Apple's stock price reflects concerns about supply chain disruptions, competition, and market saturation in certain product categories. Additionally, Apple's exposure to global markets means that it is affected by geopolitical tensions and regulatory changes, particularly in key regions like China. Despite these challenges, Apple's strong balance sheet, innovative product pipeline, and expanding services business provide a solid foundation for future growth.

The technology sector's recent experiences underscore the complexities and uncertainties that companies face in an ever-evolving market. While the promise of new technologies like AI continues to drive interest and investment, the risks associated with overvaluation, competitive pressures, and broader economic factors cannot be ignored. The case studies of Nvidia, Intel, Amazon, and Apple provide insights into how different companies navigate these challenges and capitalize on emerging opportunities.

As the technology landscape continues to evolve, it will be crucial for investors, policymakers, and industry participants to stay informed and adaptable. The future of the tech sector will likely be shaped by a combination of technological advancements, regulatory developments, and macroeconomic trends. In this dynamic environment, understanding the nuances and complexities of the sector will be key to making informed decisions and identifying the opportunities and risks that lie ahead.

Chapter 4: Global Ripple Effects

Market Reactions in Europe and Asia

The turbulence in U.S. stock markets inevitably reverberated across global financial markets, prompting significant reactions in Europe and Asia. These regions, deeply interconnected with the American economy through trade, investment, and financial channels, experienced substantial market movements as investors reacted to shifting economic indicators and sentiments.

In Europe, major stock indices such as the FTSE 100 in London, the DAX in Frankfurt, and the CAC 40 in Paris faced sharp declines. These indices, which encompass a wide range of industries from financial services to manufacturing, reflect the broader economic landscape of the continent. The declines were precipitated by fears of a slowing global economy and the potential impact on European companies, many of which rely heavily on exports to the United States and other regions.

The downturn in European markets was also influenced by specific regional factors. The energy sector, for example, faced headwinds due to fluctuating oil and gas prices, which were affected by geopolitical tensions and supply chain issues. Financial stocks were under pressure as concerns about interest rate changes and economic stability prompted caution among investors. Additionally, ongoing challenges such as Brexit-related uncertainties and economic disparities within the European Union contributed to a cautious market environment.

In Asia, the reaction was similarly pronounced. The Nikkei 225 in Japan, the Hang Seng Index in Hong

Kong, and other major indices across the region experienced significant losses. The sharp decline in the Nikkei, in particular, highlighted Japan's sensitivity to global economic shifts, given its status as a major exporter and its integration into global supply chains. The Japanese market's reaction was further exacerbated by the strengthening yen, which posed challenges for export-oriented companies.

Other Asian markets, including those in South Korea, Taiwan, and China, also saw notable declines. The interconnectedness of these economies means that shifts in one part of the region can have cascading effects. For instance, South Korea and Taiwan, both key players in the semiconductor industry, faced uncertainties due to changing demand and potential disruptions in supply chains. Meanwhile, China's market dynamics were influenced by a combination of domestic economic policies and external pressures, including trade relations with the United States.

The response of Asian markets was also shaped by broader macroeconomic concerns, such as inflationary pressures and changing monetary policies. Central banks across the region faced difficult choices, balancing the need to support economic growth with the imperative to manage inflation and maintain financial stability. The interplay between these factors created a complex and uncertain environment for investors, contributing to the volatility observed in the markets.

The Strengthening Yen and Japan's Economic Challenges

The Japanese yen's appreciation against major currencies, particularly the U.S. dollar, has been a critical development with far-reaching implications for Japan's economy. A stronger yen can have both positive and negative effects, influencing trade, investment, and economic growth in various ways.

One of the immediate consequences of a strengthening yen is its impact on Japan's export-driven economy. Japanese products become more expensive for foreign buyers, potentially reducing demand for exports. This poses a significant challenge for Japanese companies, particularly those in key industries such as automotive, electronics, and machinery, which rely heavily on overseas sales. A decrease in export volumes can lead to reduced revenues, lower profits, and potentially even job cuts, affecting the broader economy.

The appreciation of the yen also has implications for Japan's financial markets. A stronger currency can attract foreign investors seeking safer assets, such as Japanese government bonds. This influx of capital can drive up bond prices and lower yields, affecting the returns on investments. For Japanese investors, the currency's strength can impact the value of their foreign investments, as the returns in yen terms may be reduced when converted back from other currencies.

The Bank of Japan (BOJ), the country's central bank, plays a crucial role in managing these economic challenges. The BOJ's monetary policy decisions, including interest rate adjustments and asset purchase programs, are closely watched by investors and policymakers. In recent years, the BOJ has maintained an ultra-loose monetary policy to stimulate economic growth and combat deflation. However, the rising yen complicates these efforts, as it can counteract the intended stimulative effects by reducing export competitiveness and import prices.

Inflation, or the lack thereof, has been a persistent issue in Japan. The country has struggled with low inflation and occasional deflation for decades, which can stifle economic growth by encouraging consumers to delay purchases in anticipation of lower prices. The recent increase in inflation, driven in part by rising energy costs and supply chain disruptions, poses a new challenge. The BOJ must carefully navigate the balance between supporting economic growth and managing inflationary pressures, particularly in the context of a strengthening yen.

The broader economic landscape in Japan is further complicated by structural challenges, such as an aging population and a shrinking workforce. These demographic trends put pressure on the economy's potential growth rate and strain public finances, as the government must allocate resources for healthcare and pensions. The combination of these structural issues with cyclical economic challenges creates a complex environment for policymakers and businesses alike.

Contagion Fears: A Global Perspective

The interconnected nature of the global economy means that economic disturbances in one region can quickly spread to others, a phenomenon often referred to as "contagion." The recent market turmoil has sparked concerns about such contagion, with investors and policymakers closely monitoring the potential for spillover effects across borders.

One of the primary channels through which contagion can occur is through financial markets. As investors react to economic developments, they may adjust their portfolios, leading to capital flows across countries and asset classes. For example, a sell-off in U.S. stocks can lead to similar actions in other markets, as investors seek to rebalance their portfolios and reduce exposure to perceived risks. This can create a domino effect, with market declines in one region triggering similar movements elsewhere.

Another channel is through trade and investment linkages. The global economy is deeply interconnected, with countries relying on each other for goods, services, and capital. A slowdown in one major economy can reduce demand for imports, affecting exporters in other countries. For instance, a weakening U.S. economy can lead to reduced demand for European and Asian products, impacting those regions' export sectors. Similarly, changes in investment flows, such as reductions in foreign direct investment, can affect economic activity in host countries.

The recent market disturbances have also highlighted vulnerabilities in emerging markets. These economies are often more susceptible to external shocks due to factors such as smaller financial markets, higher debt levels, and reliance on foreign investment. As risk aversion increases, investors may withdraw capital from these markets, leading to currency depreciation, rising borrowing costs, and financial instability. The potential for contagion is particularly concerning in emerging markets with large external debt burdens or fragile financial systems.

Contagion fears are further exacerbated by the role of global supply chains. Many industries, including technology, automotive, and manufacturing, rely on complex networks of suppliers and producers spread across multiple countries. Disruptions in one part of the supply chain can have cascading effects, leading to production delays, shortages of key components, and increased costs. The recent challenges in the semiconductor industry, for instance, have highlighted the vulnerabilities of global supply chains and the potential for disruptions to spread across industries and regions.

Policymakers and international organizations play a crucial role in managing and mitigating the risks of contagion. Coordinated policy responses, such as central bank interventions and fiscal stimulus measures, can help stabilize markets and support economic activity. Additionally, international institutions like the International Monetary Fund (IMF) and the World Bank provide financial assistance and technical support to countries facing economic challenges. These efforts can help contain the spread of economic disturbances and support global stability.

However, the effectiveness of these measures depends on a range of factors, including the speed and scale of the response, the specific economic conditions in affected countries, and the willingness of governments to cooperate. The complex and interconnected nature of the global economy means that managing contagion requires a nuanced and coordinated approach, taking into account the unique circumstances and challenges faced by different countries.

The recent market turmoil has highlighted the global nature of economic challenges and the potential for contagion across regions. The reactions in Europe and Asia, the strengthening yen and its impact on Japan, and the broader fears of contagion underscore the interconnectedness of the global economy. As we move forward, understanding and addressing these global ripple effects will be crucial for maintaining economic stability and fostering sustainable growth. The next chapters will explore these themes in greater depth, examining the specific impacts on different sectors and regions, and considering potential policy responses and future scenarios.

Chapter 5: Investors' Reactions and Strategies

Short-Term vs. Long-Term Investor Behavior

The recent volatility in global financial markets has highlighted contrasting approaches among investors, particularly in terms of their time horizons and risk appetites. Understanding these dynamics is crucial for comprehending market movements and predicting future trends.

Short-Term Investor Behavior:

Short-term investors, often referred to as traders, are characterized by their focus on exploiting short-term price movements to generate quick profits. These investors typically rely on technical analysis, market trends, and short-term indicators to make trading decisions. The recent market volatility provided ample opportunities for short-term traders to capitalize on rapid price fluctuations, as fear and uncertainty gripped the markets.

One common strategy among short-term investors during periods of volatility is to engage in active trading, buying and selling securities frequently in response to changing market conditions. This strategy can involve leveraging financial instruments such as derivatives to amplify returns or hedge against potential losses. However, it also exposes traders to heightened risks, as market volatility can lead to significant and sudden price swings.

Short-term investors may also employ defensive strategies, such as placing stop-loss orders to limit potential losses or using options to hedge against downside risk. These tactics aim to protect capital during periods of uncertainty while still allowing for potential profit-taking opportunities. The ability to react quickly to market developments and adapt trading strategies accordingly is a hallmark of short-term investor behavior.

Despite the potential for high returns, short-term trading is not without its challenges. It requires a deep understanding of market dynamics, technical analysis skills, and the ability to manage emotions effectively. The psychological aspect of trading, including fear and greed, can influence decision-making and impact trading outcomes. Moreover, short-term trading strategies may not be suitable for all investors, particularly those with a long-term investment horizon or a lower tolerance for risk.

Long-Term Investor Behavior:

In contrast to short-term traders, long-term investors take a more strategic and patient approach to investing. These investors focus on fundamental analysis, assessing the intrinsic value of securities based on factors such as earnings growth, market position, and management quality. Long-term investors typically aim to build wealth over time through capital appreciation and dividend income, rather than seeking quick gains from market fluctuations.

During periods of market volatility, long-term investors often adhere to their investment principles and resist the temptation to react impulsively to short-term noise. They recognize that market downturns are a normal part of the investment cycle and may present buying opportunities for quality assets at discounted prices. Warren Buffett famously advises, "Be fearful when others are greedy and greedy when others are fearful," reflecting the contrarian mindset often adopted by long-term investors.

One key strategy employed by long-term investors is dollar-cost averaging, whereby they invest a fixed amount of money at regular intervals, regardless of market conditions. This approach helps mitigate the impact of market volatility by spreading investment purchases over time. It allows investors to benefit from both market downturns (when prices are lower) and upturns (when prices are higher), potentially reducing the overall average cost per share.

Another hallmark of long-term investing is portfolio diversification. By spreading investments across different asset classes, industries, and geographic regions, long-term investors seek to reduce the risk of significant losses from any single investment. Diversification can enhance portfolio resilience during market downturns and provide opportunities for growth in diverse economic conditions.

Long-term investors also prioritize fundamental research and due diligence when selecting investments. They focus on factors such as corporate governance, competitive advantages, and sustainability practices to assess the long-term viability and growth potential of companies. This disciplined approach helps long-term investors weather short-term volatility and stay focused on their investment objectives.

The Role of Institutional Investors

Institutional investors play a pivotal role in global financial markets, wielding significant influence due to their size, resources, and investment mandates. These investors include pension funds, mutual funds, hedge funds, insurance companies, and sovereign wealth funds, among others. Understanding their behavior and strategies is essential for comprehending market dynamics and the transmission of economic shocks.

Types of Institutional Investors:

1. Pension Funds: Pension funds manage retirement savings for millions of individuals and invest in a diversified portfolio of assets to generate returns over the long term. They are guided by fiduciary responsibilities to maximize returns while managing risks prudently.

2. Mutual Funds: Mutual funds pool money from multiple investors to invest in stocks, bonds, and other securities. They offer diversification and professional management, making them popular among retail investors seeking exposure to various asset classes.

3. Hedge Funds: Hedge funds pursue aggressive investment strategies to achieve high returns, often using leverage and derivatives. They have greater flexibility compared to traditional funds but also carry higher risks and fees.

4. Insurance Companies: Insurance companies invest premiums received from policyholders in a range of assets to meet future obligations, such as claims payments. They prioritize stability and income generation while managing liquidity and regulatory requirements.

5. Sovereign Wealth Funds: Sovereign wealth funds manage government-owned assets and invest globally to generate wealth for future generations or stabilize economies. They play a strategic role in international markets due to their long-term investment horizon and substantial capital base.

Institutional Investor Strategies:

Institutional investors employ diverse strategies tailored to their investment objectives, risk tolerance, and market conditions. These strategies can range from passive index investing to active stock picking and alternative investments.

1. Passive Index Investing: Institutional investors may replicate market indices, such as the S&P 500 or FTSE 100, by investing in exchange-traded funds (ETFs) or index funds. This approach aims to achieve broad market exposure and diversification at a low cost, reflecting a belief in market efficiency.

2. Active Management: Some institutional investors engage in active management, seeking to outperform benchmark indices through research, analysis, and selective investments. Active managers may capitalize on market inefficiencies, sector rotations, or company-specific opportunities to generate alpha (excess returns).

3. Alternative Investments: Hedge funds and certain institutional investors allocate capital to alternative investments, such as private equity, venture capital, real estate, and commodities. These assets offer diversification benefits and the potential for high returns but also entail higher risks and longer investment horizons.

4. Risk Management: Institutional investors prioritize risk management strategies to protect capital and minimize losses during market downturns. This includes portfolio diversification, hedging with derivatives, and stress testing to assess potential vulnerabilities.

5. Corporate Governance and Engagement: Institutional investors often engage with companies on corporate governance issues, sustainability practices, and strategic decisions. They may vote on shareholder resolutions, advocate for board accountability, and promote responsible business practices.

Mitigation Strategies in a Volatile Market

Navigating volatile markets requires investors to adopt prudent mitigation strategies aimed at preserving capital, managing risk, and seizing opportunities amid uncertainty. These strategies encompass a range of approaches tailored to individual risk profiles and investment objectives.

Diversification: One of the fundamental principles of risk management is portfolio diversification. By spreading investments across different asset classes, industries, and geographic regions, investors can reduce the impact of market downturns on their overall portfolio. Diversification helps mitigate concentration risk and enhances portfolio resilience in diverse economic conditions.

Asset Allocation: Asset allocation involves determining the optimal mix of stocks, bonds, cash, and alternative investments based on an investor's risk tolerance, time horizon, and financial goals. Strategic asset allocation aims to balance growth potential with downside protection, adjusting allocations periodically in response to changing market conditions.

Risk Management Techniques: Investors utilize various risk management techniques to protect capital and minimize losses during market turbulence. These techniques may include setting stop-loss orders to limit downside risk, hedging with options or futures contracts, and employing tactical asset allocation strategies based on market indicators.

Cash Reserves: Maintaining adequate cash reserves provides liquidity and flexibility to capitalize on investment opportunities during market downturns. Cash reserves can be deployed to purchase undervalued assets, rebalance portfolios, or meet short-term liquidity needs without having to sell investments at unfavorable prices.

Long-Term Focus: Adopting a long-term investment horizon helps investors withstand short-term market fluctuations and capitalize on compounding returns over time. Long-term investors focus on fundamental analysis, quality of investments, and sustainable growth prospects rather than reacting impulsively to market volatility.

Stress Testing and Scenario Analysis: Conducting stress tests and scenario analysis helps investors assess the resilience of their portfolios to potential economic shocks and extreme market conditions. By simulating different scenarios, investors can identify vulnerabilities, adjust risk exposures, and enhance portfolio preparedness.

Active Monitoring and Adjustment: Active monitoring of market trends, economic indicators, and geopolitical developments enables investors to make informed decisions and adjust portfolios proactively. Staying informed about market dynamics and maintaining a disciplined investment approach are critical during periods of volatility.

Behavioral Discipline: Managing behavioral biases, such as fear and greed, is essential for maintaining discipline and making rational investment decisions. Avoiding emotional reactions to market fluctuations and adhering to a predetermined investment strategy can help investors stay on course and achieve long-term financial objectives.

Investors' reactions and strategies during periods of market volatility reflect diverse approaches shaped by individual preferences, risk tolerance, and investment objectives. Short-term traders capitalize on rapid price movements, while long-term investors prioritize fundamental analysis and strategic asset allocation. Institutional investors, with their significant capital and influence, play a pivotal role in shaping market dynamics and transmitting economic shocks globally. Mitigation strategies such as diversification, asset allocation, risk management, and behavioral discipline are essential for navigating volatile markets and achieving long-term financial success.

Understanding the interplay between investor behavior, institutional strategies, and market dynamics provides valuable insights into the resilience of global financial markets and the potential for sustainable growth amid uncertainty. The next chapters will delve deeper into sector-specific impacts, policy responses, and future outlooks, exploring how these factors shape the evolving landscape of global finance.

Chapter 6: Analyzing the U.S. Economic Outlook

Growth Prospects and Recession Risks

The U.S. economic outlook is currently a focal point for policymakers, investors, and analysts, given the interplay of various factors influencing growth prospects and recession risks. Evaluating these aspects requires a comprehensive analysis of recent economic data, structural dynamics, and external pressures.

Economic Growth Trends:

The U.S. economy has experienced a pattern of growth characterized by periods of expansion followed by occasional slowdowns. Recent data suggests that while growth remains positive, it faces several challenges. Gross Domestic Product (GDP) growth, a critical indicator of economic performance, has shown variability in recent quarters. For instance, the economy expanded at an annual rate of 2.8% in the three months ending in June, reflecting a strong performance compared to other developed economies. However, the consistency of this growth rate is under scrutiny, especially given recent weak jobs data and other economic indicators.

Consumer spending, a significant driver of economic activity, remains robust. This resilience is supported by factors such as rising wages and a historically low unemployment rate. Nevertheless, consumer confidence can be volatile and sensitive to economic fluctuations, impacting spending patterns. Retail sales and consumer sentiment surveys offer insights into the health of consumer spending, which is crucial for maintaining economic momentum.

Business investment trends present a mixed picture. While some sectors continue to invest in expansion and innovation, others show caution amid uncertainties. Investment in technology and infrastructure, driven by favorable economic conditions and low interest rates, contributes positively to growth. However, uncertainties related to trade policies, regulatory changes, and geopolitical tensions can influence business confidence and investment decisions.

Labor market dynamics play a critical role in shaping economic growth. The U.S. labor market has been characterized by low unemployment rates and steady job creation. Yet, recent data indicating a slowdown in job growth and an uptick in the unemployment rate raise concerns about the sustainability of the labor market recovery. Factors such as labor force participation, wage growth, and job quality impact overall economic health and consumer spending capacity.

Inflation has become a prominent concern, with recent data showing rising prices for goods and services. The Federal Reserve's target inflation rate of around 2% aims to ensure price stability while supporting economic growth. Rising inflation could lead to higher interest rates, impacting borrowing costs and consumer spending.

Recession Risks:

Despite ongoing economic expansion, there are several risk factors that could potentially lead to a recession. Analyzing these risks involves evaluating both internal and external influences on the economy.

1. Global Economic Uncertainty: Slowing growth in major economies, trade tensions, and geopolitical risks contribute to global economic uncertainty. These factors can affect U.S. exports, supply chains, and overall business sentiment. Trade disputes and

economic slowdowns in key markets, such as China and the Eurozone, have the potential to ripple through the U.S. economy.

2. Financial Market Volatility: Financial markets have experienced significant fluctuations, reflecting investor sentiment and expectations. Volatility in stock markets, changes in bond yields, and credit market disruptions can signal potential economic stress. Financial instability often leads to tighter credit conditions and reduced consumer and business confidence.

3. Policy and Political Uncertainty: Domestic policy changes, including fiscal policies, regulatory reforms, and political developments, influence economic stability. Uncertainty surrounding policy decisions, budget allocations, and political gridlock can impact business investment, consumer confidence, and economic growth.

4. Structural Challenges: Long-term structural factors, such as demographic shifts and productivity trends, pose challenges to sustainable economic growth. An aging population, changing workforce dynamics, and productivity stagnation require strategic policy interventions to address potential growth constraints.

Assessing recession risks involves analyzing leading economic indicators, financial market trends, and policy responses. Economists and policymakers monitor a range of data to gauge the likelihood of an economic downturn and adjust policy measures accordingly.

The Federal Reserve's Dilemma

The Federal Reserve, as the central bank of the United States, faces complex challenges in navigating monetary policy to achieve its dual mandate of maximum employment and stable prices. The Fed's policy decisions have far-reaching implications for economic growth, inflation, and financial stability.

Monetary Policy Tools:

The Federal Reserve employs several key tools to influence monetary conditions and support its policy objectives:

1. Interest Rates: The Fed sets the target range for the federal funds rate, influencing short-term interest rates and borrowing costs. Lower interest rates stimulate economic activity by making borrowing cheaper for consumers and businesses. Conversely, higher rates aim to control inflation and prevent excessive risk-taking.

2. Asset Purchases: In response to economic stress or financial instability, the Fed may engage in asset purchases, including Treasury securities and

mortgage-backed securities. These purchases inject liquidity into financial markets, lower long-term interest rates, and support credit availability.

3. Forward Guidance: The Fed provides forward guidance on its policy intentions and economic outlook to influence market expectations and investor behavior. Clear communication about future policy actions helps shape market expectations and enhances transparency.

4. Regulatory Oversight: The Fed regulates and supervises financial institutions to ensure the stability and soundness of the banking system. Regulatory policies aim to mitigate systemic risks, enhance market transparency, and promote fair and efficient financial markets.

Current Policy Stance:

The Federal Reserve's policy stance has evolved in response to changing economic conditions. In the aftermath of the COVID-19 pandemic, the Fed adopted accommodative measures, including rate cuts and expanded asset purchases, to support economic recovery. As the economy has improved, the Fed has begun to shift towards a more neutral policy stance, gradually tapering asset purchases and signaling potential rate hikes.

The Fed's decisions are guided by a range of economic indicators, including GDP growth, inflation, and labor market conditions. The timing and magnitude of future interest rate changes depend on the Fed's assessment of economic data and its alignment with policy objectives.

Challenges and Considerations:

The Federal Reserve faces several challenges in navigating its policy decisions:

1. Inflation Dynamics: Balancing the goals of price stability and maximum employment requires

careful consideration of inflationary pressures. Rising inflation can prompt the Fed to raise interest rates, potentially impacting economic growth and employment.

2. Economic Uncertainty: The Fed's policy decisions are influenced by uncertainties surrounding the economic outlook, including global economic conditions, financial market stability, and domestic policy developments.

3. Financial Stability: Ensuring financial stability involves monitoring market conditions, asset valuations, and systemic risks. The Fed assesses the resilience of financial institutions and the potential impact of financial market disruptions on economic stability.

4. Communication Strategy: Effective communication is essential for guiding market expectations and enhancing transparency. The Fed's statements, press conferences, and economic

projections shape investor sentiment and influence market reactions.

Economic Policy and Political Factors

Economic policy in the United States is shaped by a complex interplay of political, institutional, and policy factors. Understanding these dynamics is crucial for analyzing the formulation and impact of economic policies on the U.S. economy.

Policy Objectives:

Economic policies aim to achieve several core objectives:

1. Promoting Full Employment: Policies are designed to reduce unemployment, increase labor force participation, and create job opportunities.

Employment growth supports consumer spending and strengthens economic stability.

2. Maintaining Price Stability: Ensuring price stability involves controlling inflation and preventing deflation. Stable prices preserve purchasing power and support long-term economic planning.

3. Fostering Economic Growth: Policies aimed at stimulating economic growth focus on enhancing productivity, innovation, and competitiveness. Investments in infrastructure, education, and research drive long-term growth.

4. Ensuring Financial Stability: Regulatory policies aim to safeguard financial markets and institutions, ensuring their stability and resilience. Oversight of financial practices and systemic risk management are key aspects of maintaining market integrity.

Political Factors:

Political dynamics play a significant role in shaping economic policy:

1. Policy Ideologies: Political ideologies influence policy preferences on issues such as taxation, government spending, and regulation. Different political perspectives lead to varying approaches to economic management and policy formulation.

2. Legislative Process: Economic policies are enacted through the legislative process involving Congress, the President, and federal agencies. Legislative debates and negotiations determine the content and implementation of economic policies.

3. Election Cycles: Political elections impact policy agendas and priorities. Changes in leadership and party control can lead to shifts in economic policy direction and implementation.

4. Public Opinion and Stakeholder Interests: Public perceptions and stakeholder interests influence policy decisions. Advocacy groups, industry associations, and labor unions play a role in shaping policy outcomes and priorities.

Implementation Challenges:

Implementing economic policies involves addressing several challenges:

1. Policy Effectiveness: Evaluating the effectiveness of policies requires analyzing economic data and assessing outcomes against policy objectives. Effective implementation and monitoring are crucial for achieving desired results.

2. Coordination and Consensus: Achieving coordination and consensus among stakeholders, policymakers, and agencies is essential for successful policy implementation. Collaboration and engagement facilitate effective policy execution.

3. Budgetary Constraints: Fiscal policies face budgetary constraints and funding priorities. Balancing spending commitments, revenue sources, and deficit management requires prudent fiscal management.

4. External Factors: External factors, such as global economic conditions and geopolitical events, can impact the effectiveness of domestic policies. Policymakers must consider these external influences when formulating and implementing economic strategies.

Analyzing the U.S. economic outlook involves evaluating growth prospects, recession risks, and the Federal Reserve's policy decisions. Understanding the impact of political and economic factors provides insights into the formulation and implementation of economic policies, highlighting the complexities and challenges faced by policymakers and stakeholders.

Chapter 7: Comparative Analysis: Global Economic Health

Comparing Major Economies: U.S., Europe, Asia

To understand the current state of the global economy, a comparative analysis of the major economic regions—the United States, Europe, and Asia—is essential. Each region possesses unique economic characteristics, challenges, and opportunities that influence their global economic standing and interconnections.

United States:

The U.S. economy, the largest in the world, has been a dominant force in global finance and trade.

Its economic performance is driven by several key factors:

1. Economic Growth: The U.S. has experienced relatively strong growth in recent years, characterized by robust consumer spending, a dynamic labor market, and significant technological innovation. However, growth rates have shown variability, influenced by domestic and global economic conditions.

2. Labor Market: The U.S. labor market is marked by a low unemployment rate, high job creation, and rising wages. The service sector dominates employment, with technology and healthcare sectors showing notable expansion. However, challenges such as income inequality and labor market mismatches persist.

3. Monetary Policy: The Federal Reserve plays a central role in U.S. economic policy, utilizing interest rates and asset purchases to manage

economic growth and inflation. Recent policy adjustments have focused on balancing economic expansion with price stability.

4. Fiscal Policy: U.S. fiscal policy includes a mix of government spending and taxation, aimed at stimulating growth and addressing social needs. The impact of fiscal policies, including stimulus measures and tax reforms, is significant in shaping economic outcomes.

5. Trade: The U.S. engages in extensive international trade, with key trading partners including China, the European Union, and Mexico. Trade policies and agreements impact economic growth, industry competitiveness, and global supply chains.

Europe:

The European economy, comprising diverse countries with varying economic conditions, faces its own set of challenges and opportunities:

1. Economic Growth: Europe has experienced moderate growth, influenced by factors such as demographic changes, economic integration, and regional disparities. While core economies like Germany and France show resilience, southern and eastern European countries face slower growth and higher unemployment rates.

2. Labor Market: Europe's labor market is characterized by varying unemployment rates across member states. Structural issues, such as labor market rigidities and skill mismatches, impact employment outcomes. Social safety nets and labor regulations also shape labor market dynamics.

3. Monetary Policy: The European Central Bank (ECB) is responsible for monetary policy across the Eurozone. The ECB's policies focus on maintaining

price stability and supporting economic growth. Recent measures include low interest rates and quantitative easing to address economic challenges.

4. Fiscal Policy: Fiscal policy in Europe is influenced by both national and EU-level decisions. Countries with high levels of public debt face constraints on fiscal policy, while efforts to promote economic convergence and stability are central to EU policy frameworks.

5. Trade: Europe is a major global trading bloc, with significant trade relationships within the EU and with external partners. Trade policies, including Brexit and trade agreements with other regions, affect Europe's economic integration and global trade dynamics.

Asia:

Asia, with its diverse economies ranging from highly developed to emerging markets, exhibits varied economic characteristics:

1. Economic Growth: Asia has been a major driver of global economic growth, particularly in countries like China and India. High rates of economic expansion, driven by industrialization, urbanization, and technological advancements, contrast with slower growth in mature economies like Japan.

2. Labor Market: Asia's labor market varies widely, from high-skilled labor in advanced economies to lower-wage labor in emerging markets. Rapid urbanization and industrialization in countries like China and India are transforming labor markets and economic structures.

3. Monetary Policy: Central banks in Asia, including the People's Bank of China (PBoC) and the Bank of Japan (BoJ), adopt monetary policies tailored to

their national contexts. Policies range from accommodative measures to stimulate growth to efforts to control inflation and stabilize currencies.

4. Fiscal Policy: Asian countries employ diverse fiscal policies to address economic priorities. Infrastructure investment, social spending, and economic stimulus measures play a role in shaping growth and stability across the region.

5. Trade: Asia is a key player in global trade, with significant trade relationships both within the region and with other parts of the world. Trade policies, regional agreements such as the Regional Comprehensive Economic Partnership (RCEP), and geopolitical factors impact trade dynamics and economic integration.

Central Bank Policies Across the Globe

Central banks play a crucial role in shaping global economic conditions through their monetary policies. Their actions influence interest rates, inflation, financial stability, and economic growth. Examining central bank policies across major economies provides insights into their respective economic strategies and challenges.

United States - Federal Reserve:

The Federal Reserve, the central bank of the United States, utilizes a range of tools to manage monetary policy:

1. Interest Rates: The Fed sets the federal funds rate, influencing short-term borrowing costs and overall monetary conditions. Adjustments to interest rates aim to balance economic growth and

inflation, with recent policy shifts reflecting concerns about economic stability and inflationary pressures.

2. Asset Purchases: The Fed engages in quantitative easing by purchasing government securities and mortgage-backed securities. These purchases inject liquidity into the financial system, support credit markets, and influence long-term interest rates.

3. Forward Guidance: The Fed uses forward guidance to communicate its future policy intentions and economic outlook. Clear communication helps manage market expectations and provides guidance on future interest rate movements.

Eurozone - European Central Bank (ECB):

The ECB manages monetary policy for the Eurozone, encompassing multiple countries using the euro:

1. Interest Rates: The ECB sets key interest rates, including the main refinancing rate and deposit facility rate. These rates impact borrowing costs, inflation, and economic activity across the Eurozone.

2. Asset Purchases: The ECB has implemented asset purchase programs, including quantitative easing, to stimulate economic growth and address low inflation. These measures involve purchasing government bonds and other assets to increase liquidity and support the economy.

3. Forward Guidance: The ECB employs forward guidance to signal its future policy stance and provide clarity to markets. Communication about policy intentions helps shape expectations and guide economic behavior.

China - People's Bank of China (PBoC):

The People's Bank of China manages monetary policy for the world's second-largest economy:

1. Interest Rates: The PBoC sets benchmark interest rates, including the one-year lending and deposit rates. These rates influence borrowing costs and credit conditions within China.

2. Reserve Requirements: The PBoC uses reserve requirement ratios to regulate the amount of reserves banks must hold. Adjustments to reserve requirements impact lending capacity and liquidity in the banking system.

3. Currency Policy: The PBoC manages the value of the renminbi (RMB) through exchange rate policies and interventions. The currency's value impacts trade competitiveness and capital flows.

Japan - Bank of Japan (BoJ):

The Bank of Japan is responsible for monetary policy in Japan, a mature and developed economy:

1. Interest Rates: The BoJ sets short-term interest rates, including the policy rate and negative interest rate policy (NIRP). These measures aim to stimulate economic activity and address low inflation.

2. Asset Purchases: The BoJ engages in extensive asset purchases, including government bonds and exchange-traded funds (ETFs). These purchases support financial markets and enhance liquidity.

3. Forward Guidance: The BoJ uses forward guidance to communicate its policy intentions and provide market guidance. Clear communication helps shape expectations and influence economic behavior.

The Role of Trade and Geopolitical Tensions

Trade and geopolitical tensions significantly impact global economic dynamics, influencing trade flows, investment decisions, and economic stability. Examining these factors provides insights into their effects on major economies and the global economy as a whole.

Trade Dynamics:

1. Global Trade Flows: International trade is a critical component of global economic growth, with major economies relying on exports and imports for economic activity. Trade flows impact supply chains, commodity prices, and economic performance.

2. Trade Agreements: Trade agreements, such as bilateral, regional, and multilateral agreements,

shape trade relationships and market access. Agreements like the US-Mexico-Canada Agreement (USMCA) and the Regional Comprehensive Economic Partnership (RCEP) influence trade patterns and economic integration.

3. Tariffs and Trade Barriers: Trade policies, including tariffs, quotas, and non-tariff barriers, affect trade flows and economic competitiveness. Trade disputes, such as those between the U.S. and China, can lead to economic disruptions and impact global supply chains.

Geopolitical Tensions:

1. Political Risks: Geopolitical tensions, including conflicts, territorial disputes, and political instability, can disrupt economic activity and impact investor confidence. Regional conflicts and geopolitical uncertainties influence global markets and economic stability.

2. Economic Sanctions: Economic sanctions imposed by countries or international bodies can affect trade, investment, and economic relations. Sanctions targeting specific countries or sectors can disrupt global supply chains and impact economic performance.

3. Strategic Alliances: Geopolitical alliances and partnerships play a role in shaping economic policies and trade relationships. Strategic alliances, such as those between major economics and regional blocs, influence global economic dynamics and policy coordination.

Impact on Major Economies:

1. United States: Trade policies and geopolitical tensions impact U.S. economic performance, with implications for trade balances, supply chains, and investment decisions. Trade disputes and geopolitical developments influence U.S. economic growth and global leadership.

2. Europe: Europe's economic performance is influenced by trade relationships and geopolitical factors. Trade agreements, Brexit, and geopolitical tensions affect economic integration, trade flows, and regional stability.

3. Asia: Asia's economic performance is shaped by trade dynamics and geopolitical tensions, particularly in key economies like China and Japan. Trade relationships, regional conflicts, and geopolitical developments impact economic growth and stability.

A comparative analysis of global economic health highlights the diverse economic characteristics, challenges, and opportunities across major economies. Central bank policies, trade dynamics, and geopolitical tensions play a significant role in shaping global economic conditions. Understanding these factors provides valuable insights into the interconnected nature of the global economy and the complexities of navigating economic uncertainties and opportunities. The subsequent chapter will delve into the future outlook and potential scenarios for the global economy, offering insights into emerging trends and developments.

Chapter 8: Lessons Learned and Future Predictions

Historical Comparisons: Previous Market Crashes

To gain insights into the current market dynamics and anticipate future trends, it's valuable to examine past market crashes. Historical comparisons provide context, reveal recurring patterns, and offer lessons on resilience and recovery.

The Great Depression (1929-1939):

The Great Depression is one of the most severe economic crises in history. Triggered by the stock market crash of October 1929, it led to a prolonged period of economic contraction. Key factors included excessive speculation, overleveraged investments, and a banking crisis.

- Market Collapse: The stock market crash of 1929 saw the Dow Jones Industrial Average (DJIA) fall dramatically, with significant declines in share prices. This collapse precipitated a broader economic downturn, characterized by widespread unemployment and deflation.
- Policy Responses: The U.S. government and the Federal Reserve initially responded with insufficient measures. It wasn't until the New Deal programs and increased federal spending that recovery began. These included reforms aimed at stabilizing the financial system and providing economic relief.
- Lessons Learned: The Great Depression underscored the importance of regulatory oversight, fiscal intervention, and social safety nets. It demonstrated how unchecked financial practices could lead to systemic failures and the need for robust economic policies to stabilize markets.

The Dot-Com Bubble (1999-2000):

The late 1990s saw a surge in technology stocks, driven by speculative investments in internet and technology companies. The bubble burst in 2000, leading to a sharp decline in stock prices and a subsequent economic slowdown.

- Speculative Frenzy: The dot-com bubble was marked by inflated valuations of technology companies, driven by the promise of revolutionary internet technologies and growth potential. Many companies with unproven business models saw their stock prices soar.
- Market Correction: The bursting of the bubble led to a severe market correction, with the Nasdaq Composite Index falling significantly. This correction revealed the risks of excessive speculation and the vulnerability of overvalued assets.
- Lessons Learned: The dot-com bubble highlighted the dangers of speculative investing and the

importance of due diligence and realistic valuation assessments. It emphasized the need for investors to scrutinize business fundamentals rather than chase short-term gains.

The Global Financial Crisis (2007-2008):

The global financial crisis, triggered by the collapse of Lehman Brothers and the subprime mortgage crisis, led to widespread financial turmoil and economic recession. It revealed systemic risks within the financial system and the global interconnectedness of markets.

- Crisis Origins: The crisis stemmed from high-risk lending practices, excessive leverage, and a housing bubble. Financial products linked to mortgage defaults led to significant losses for financial institutions and a liquidity crisis.
- Policy Responses: In response, central banks and governments implemented aggressive measures, including bailouts for financial institutions,

monetary easing, and fiscal stimulus packages. These interventions aimed to stabilize financial markets and support economic recovery.

- Lessons Learned: The global financial crisis underscored the importance of financial regulation, risk management, and transparency. It demonstrated the need for systemic oversight and the role of monetary and fiscal policy in mitigating economic shocks.

The COVID-19 Pandemic (2020-Present):

The COVID-19 pandemic caused a sharp and unprecedented market downturn in early 2020. The crisis led to global economic disruptions, highlighting vulnerabilities in the global economy and the rapid adaptation of financial markets.

- Pandemic Impact: The pandemic led to widespread lockdowns, travel restrictions, and disruptions to global supply chains. Financial markets experienced extreme volatility, with sharp declines followed by rapid recoveries driven by unprecedented fiscal and monetary measures.

- Policy Responses: Governments and central banks implemented extensive stimulus measures, including direct payments, unemployment benefits, and monetary easing. These actions aimed to cushion the economic impact and support recovery.

- Lessons Learned: The COVID-19 crisis highlighted the importance of agility in policy responses and the need for effective public health measures. It underscored the interconnectedness of global economies and the rapid adaptation required to address emerging crises.

What Investors Can Learn from the Recent Tumble

The recent market downturn has offered valuable lessons for investors, emphasizing the importance of strategic planning, risk management, and adaptability.

1. Diversification:

Diversification remains a fundamental principle for managing investment risk. The recent market turbulence underscored the importance of spreading investments across various asset classes, sectors, and geographic regions.

- Mitigating Risk: Diversification helps mitigate the impact of market declines in specific sectors or regions. By holding a range of investments, investors can reduce the risk associated with individual assets and enhance overall portfolio stability.
- Asset Allocation: Strategic asset allocation, considering factors such as risk tolerance and investment horizon, helps achieve a balanced portfolio. Diversifying across equities, bonds, real

estate, and alternative assets can enhance resilience during market downturns.

2. **Long-Term Perspective:**

Maintaining a long-term investment perspective is crucial for navigating market volatility and achieving financial goals. Short-term market fluctuations can be unsettling, but a long-term approach helps investors stay focused on their objectives.

- Avoiding Panic Selling: The recent market tumble highlighted the risks of panic selling and emotional decision-making. Investors who remained committed to their long-term strategies were better positioned to benefit from subsequent recoveries.
- Compounding Growth: Long-term investing allows for the compounding of returns, benefiting from the growth of investments over time. Staying invested through market fluctuations can enhance

the potential for achieving long-term financial goals.

3. Risk Management:

Effective risk management strategies are essential for navigating uncertain market conditions. Investors need to assess and manage various risks, including market, credit, and liquidity risks.

- Stress Testing: Conducting stress tests on investment portfolios helps evaluate their resilience to different market scenarios. Understanding potential vulnerabilities enables investors to make informed decisions and adjust strategies as needed.
- Stop-Loss Orders: Implementing stop-loss orders can help limit losses during market downturns. These orders automatically sell assets when they reach a predetermined price, protecting against significant declines.

4. Staying Informed:

Keeping abreast of market developments, economic indicators, and policy changes is vital for informed investment decisions. Staying informed allows investors to anticipate potential risks and opportunities.

- Research and Analysis: Conducting thorough research and analysis of market trends, company fundamentals, and economic conditions helps investors make informed decisions. Regularly reviewing and updating investment strategies based on new information is crucial.
- Expert Advice: Seeking advice from financial professionals and advisors can provide valuable insights and guidance. Professional expertise can help investors navigate complex market conditions and develop tailored investment strategies.

5. **Flexibility and Adaptability:**

Flexibility and adaptability are key to responding effectively to changing market conditions. The recent market downturn emphasized the need for investors to adjust strategies and adapt to evolving economic environments.

- Adjusting Portfolios: Rebalancing investment portfolios based on changing market conditions and personal circumstances helps maintain alignment with financial goals. Adjusting asset allocations and investment choices can enhance portfolio resilience.
- Opportunistic Investing: Market downturns can present opportunities for value investing and long-term growth. Identifying undervalued assets and opportunities for strategic investments can benefit investors in recovering markets.

Future Market Trends and Predictions

Anticipating future market trends involves analyzing current economic conditions, technological advancements, and geopolitical developments. While predictions are inherently uncertain, several key trends are likely to shape the future economic landscape.

1. **Technological Innovation:**

Technological innovation will continue to drive economic growth and transformation across various sectors. Emerging technologies, such as artificial intelligence (AI), blockchain, and renewable energy, are poised to reshape industries and create new opportunities.

- AI and Automation: AI and automation technologies are expected to enhance productivity, efficiency, and innovation. These technologies will impact labor markets, business models, and economic growth, driving new investment opportunities.

- Green Technology: The transition to renewable energy and sustainable technologies is likely to accelerate, driven by environmental concerns and policy initiatives. Investments in green technology and clean energy are expected to grow, shaping future economic trends.

2. **Demographic Changes:**

Demographic shifts, including aging populations and changing workforce dynamics, will influence economic patterns and policy priorities. Understanding these changes is essential for anticipating future economic challenges and opportunities.

- Aging Populations: Many developed economies are experiencing aging populations, leading to increased demand for healthcare, retirement services, and changes in labor market dynamics. Addressing these challenges will require policy adjustments and innovation.

- Youthful Demographics: Emerging economies with youthful populations may experience accelerated economic growth and increased consumer demand. Harnessing the potential of young populations will be critical for driving future economic development.

3. **Globalization and Trade:**

Globalization and trade dynamics will continue to shape economic growth and international relations. Trade policies, regional agreements, and geopolitical tensions will influence global trade flows and economic integration.

- Trade Agreements: Evolving trade agreements and partnerships will impact global trade patterns and economic relationships. Regional agreements, such as the RCEP, and geopolitical developments will shape trade dynamics and market access.
- Supply Chain Resilience: The COVID-19 pandemic highlighted vulnerabilities in global supply chains.

Future trends may focus on enhancing supply chain resilience, diversifying sources, and adopting technology to mitigate disruptions.

4. Geopolitical Developments:

Geopolitical developments, including international conflicts, political instability, and shifting alliances, will influence global economic conditions and investment strategies.

- Geopolitical Risks: Ongoing geopolitical tensions and conflicts may impact market stability and investor confidence. Monitoring geopolitical developments and assessing potential risks will be essential for navigating future economic uncertainties.
- Strategic Alliances: Changes in geopolitical alliances and regional cooperation will influence economic policies and trade relationships. Strategic alliances and international collaborations will play a role in shaping global economic trends.

5. Economic Policy and Regulation:

Economic policies and regulatory frameworks will continue to evolve, impacting market dynamics and investment environments. Policymakers will address emerging challenges and priorities through fiscal, monetary, and regulatory measures

- Monetary Policy: Central banks will adapt monetary policies in response to changing economic conditions, inflationary pressures, and growth prospects. Policy decisions will influence interest rates, liquidity, and financial markets.
- Fiscal Policy: Governments will implement fiscal policies to address economic challenges, support recovery, and promote growth. Investments in infrastructure, social programs, and economic stimulus measures will shape future economic outcomes.

Examining historical market crashes, learning from recent market downturns, and anticipating future trends provides valuable insights into navigating the complexities of the global economy. Understanding past crises, applying lessons learned, and staying informed about emerging trends will help investors and policymakers adapt to changing economic conditions and seize opportunities for growth. As we move forward, a combination of strategic planning, risk management, and adaptability will be crucial for navigating the evolving economic landscape and achieving long-term success.

www.ingramcontent.com/pod-product-compliance
Lightning Source LLC
Chambersburg PA
CBHW071937210526
45479CB00002B/714